At the Dump

The Dump

Written by Claire Llewellyn
Illustrated by Ley Honor Roberts

Collins

We went to the dump with Dad.

paper

wood

glass

leaves

cardboard

We took paper, wood, glass, cardboard and leaves.

We took the paper ...

4

... and put it in here.

We took the wood ...

... and put it in here.

We took the glass ...

... and put it in here.

We took the cardboard ...

... and put it in here.

The Dump

Opening Times:
8:00 am to 8:00 pm

We took the leaves ...

12

Leaves

... and put them in here.

At the Dump

Paper

Leaves

Wood

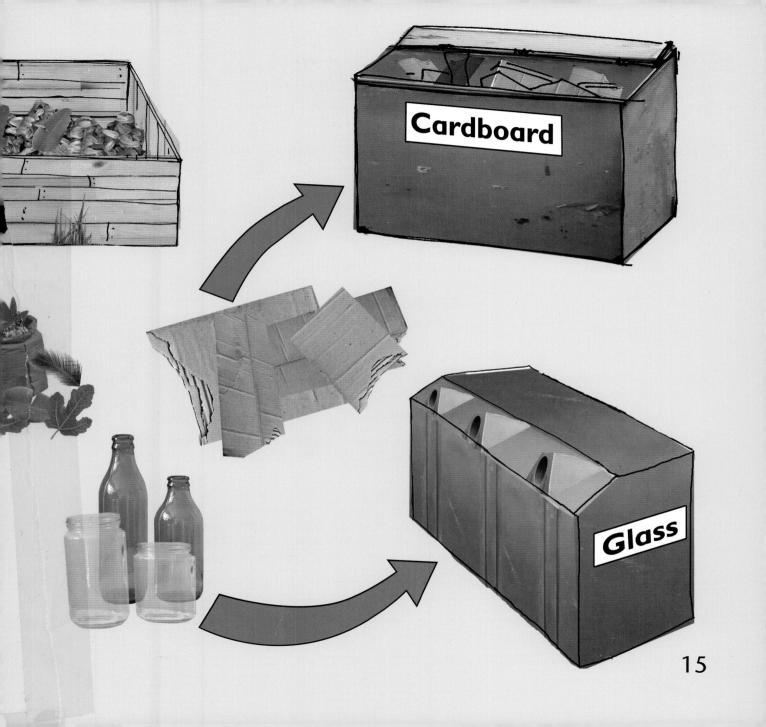

Cardboard

Glass

Ideas for reading

Written by Kelley Taylor
Educational Consultant

Learning objectives: track the text in the right order; pointing while reading and one-to-one matching; use a variety of cues when reading to work out unfamiliar words; read on sight high frequency words; recognising phonemes in initial position; in groups, ask and answer questions, make contributions, offer suggestions and take turns

Curriculum links: Knowledge and Understanding of the World: Find out about their environment

High frequency words: we, went, to, the, Dad, and, it, in

Interest words: dump, with, took, paper, wood, glass, cardboard, leaves, put, here, them

Word count: 59

Resources: Classroom bin

Getting started

- Show the classroom rubbish bin as a prop and discuss what we do to the rubbish we throw away.

- Look together at the cover of the book, and the blurb and discuss what the book is about. Introduce the word 'recycling', explain briefly what it means, and how it benefits the environment.

- Ask the children to read the title together, and observe and prompt for one-to-one matching.

- Walk through the pages and discuss what is happening on each page, up to p13. Point out the words and phrases that are repeated on each page, and check the children are happy reading the ellipses across the page spreads.

Reading and responding

- Ask the children to read aloud and independently up to p13. Observe, prompt and praise correct one-to-one matching, especially when a child has re-read to clarify meaning. Observe cross-checking from print to picture and back again and using initial phonemes to identify words.

- Discuss what they can see at the dump. Why are the family putting their rubbish in separate containers? (to help recycling).

- Ask children to check *Does that sound right?* as they read, particularly on pp12—13 where they might read, 'We took the leaves and put it in here'.

- Ask the children in pairs to look at pp14—15 and to recount what happened at the dump.